PARKOUR
THE ART OF FREER

Dan Edwardes
Parkour Generations

An Hachette UK Company
www.hachette.co.uk

First published in Great Britain in 2009 by TickTock, a division of Octopus Publishing Group Ltd,
Endeavour House, 189 Shaftesbury Avenue, London, WC2H 8JY.

www.octopusbooks.co.uk
Copyright © Octopus Publishing Group Ltd 2009

ISBN 978 1 84696 936 2

A CIP catalogue record for this book is available from the British Library

With thanks to series editors Honor Head and Jean Coppendale
Thank you to Lorraine Petersen and the members of nasen

Printed and bound in China
10 9 8 7 6 5 4 3 2 1

Picture credits (t=top; b=bottom; c=centre; l=left; r=right):
Big Pictures: 23. Gareth Brown/Corbis: OFC. Andy Day: 1, 4, 5, 6, 7r, 8, 9, 10, 11t, 11b, 12-13, 14, 15, 17, 18, 19, 20, 22, 24, 25, 28-29. Paul Holmes: 31 (both). Parkour Generations: 7l, 7c. Shutterstock: 2-3, 7 (background), 8-9 (background), 10-11 (background), 14-15 (background), 16 (background),19 (background), 21, 23 (background), 26-27 (all).

Every effort has been made to trace the copyright holders, and we apologize in advance for any unintentional omissions. We would be pleased to insert the appropriate acknowledgments in any subsequent edition of this publication.

CONTENTS

WARNING!

The parkour moves featured in this book have been performed by people who are experienced professionals, or by people who have had professional training in parkour. Neither the publisher nor the author shall be liable for any bodily harm or damage to property that may happen as a result of trying the parkour moves in this book.

CHAPTER 1 | PARKOUR!

Dynamic.
Explosive.
Powerful.

Precise.
This is parkour!

Ghosting through the city.
Running and leaping.
Overcoming any obstacle in your path.
Never stopping. Always moving.

Parkour is an art of movement. It explores the
incredible potential of your body and your mind.

CHAPTER 2

HISTORY OF PARKOUR

Parkour was created by a group of young men in France in the 1980s and 1990s.

Parkour's first name was *Art du Deplacement*. In English this means the "Art of Displacement".

Displacement means getting from one place to another using only your own body.

The name later changed to "parkour".
In the UK it was also called "freerunning".

The founders of parkour called their group "Yamakasi".

Three of the Yamakasi founders

Yann Hnautra

Laurent Piemontesi

Chau Belle-Dinh

Yamakasi is a word from the Lingala language in Africa. It means "strong man, strong spirit".

The group's goal was to become incredibly fit, strong and fast.

They wanted to become people who could meet any challenge.

CHAPTER 3

TRAINING

Parkour is a very difficult activity. It requires lots of training to be able to practise safely and correctly.

A parkour instructor teaches a group some basic vaults

The best way to learn is to be taught by experienced instructors.

Parkour is NOT about adrenaline rushes and taking risks.

It's quite the opposite!

Parkour is a way of mastering your own movement.
It is a way of training your body to achieve its full
potential.

You can do much more than you think.
Your body and mind can do amazing things
when properly trained.

Training is hard, but always good fun!

Parkour is about physical fitness and functional strength.

Functional strength means being able to move your body wherever you want to go. This includes being able to climb, run, jump, drop and twist.

You need to prepare your muscles and bones for these movements. This is known as "conditioning".

The best way to condition your body is to repeat natural, functional movements in the places you are going to practise in.

Parkour also requires regular physical training such as bodyweight drills.

A bodyweight drill is an exercise that develops your muscles. The exercise uses only the weight of your body, not solid weights.

You must improve your jump strength.

You must also improve your ability to absorb impact when you land.

CHAPTER 4

PARKOUR TECHNIQUES

There are as many different ways to move in parkour as there are people who practise it!

JUMPS

Parkour has many different types of jumps to learn. These include running jumps, standing jumps, drops and precision jumps.

Practitioners of parkour spend long hours practising how to take off and land well.

They train their legs to absorb the impact of the jump safely and in a controlled way.

Experienced practitioners can make very precise jumps of up to five or six metres in length.

Precision jumping practice is very important in parkour. You must be able to land in perfect balance on thin or small objects such as railings or walls.

VAULTS

A vault is a movement that allows you to move over an obstacle and keep moving.

A vault is normally used for obstacles that are at chest height.

Most vaults involve jumping over an obstacle while placing the hands on it for control and direction.

The *Saut de Chat* is one type of vault. It means the "jump of the cat". It is a good way to move over low obstacles quickly.

Practitioners dive headfirst over an obstacle. They place both hands on the obstacle. Then they bring their knees through their arms.

WALL-RUNNING

A wall-run is a way to get over a very high obstacle or wall.

Practitioners run at a wall.

They place a foot on the wall at about waist height.

Then they push up while reaching with their arms.

A good wall-run can help practitioners reach the top of a wall that is up to 5 metres high.

Wall-runs are very

explosive

movements!

ARM JUMPS

Jumping and grabbing onto an edge, such as the top of a wall, is known as a *Saut de Bras* in French. It means "arm jump" in English.

This move is also known as a "cat leap".

An arm jump is used when a wall or obstacle is too high to jump onto directly.

You must grab the top of the wall with your arms and then pull yourself up.

Arm jumps require a lot of upper body strength.

You can cover huge distances between obstacles using an arm jump.

Training for parkour takes time, so please don't rush. There are no short cuts and no secrets – just discipline.

CHAPTER 5

MENTAL CHALLENGE

Parkour is far more than just a physical discipline. Parkour challenges the mind in many ways.

You must learn to overcome your fear and inhibitions about movement.

An inhibition is a feeling that stops you from doing something.

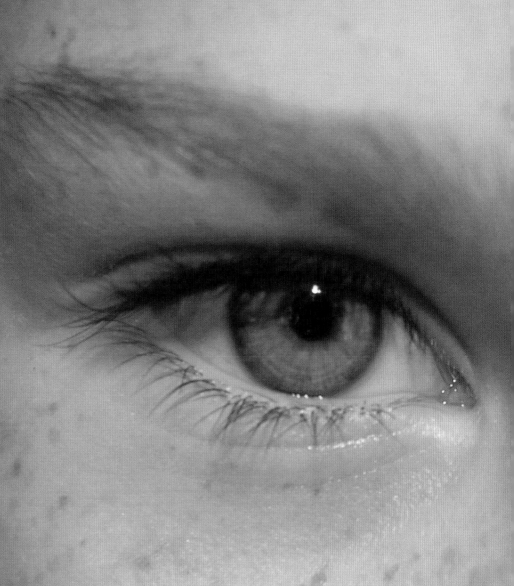

You must master your thoughts and learn to focus your attention.

Parkour builds confidence and inner control.

It helps you master yourself.

CHAPTER 6

IN THE PUBLIC EYE

In 1997 there was a movie made called *Yamakasi*. It starred the French founders of parkour.

In the movie, the Yamakasi use their amazing skills to raise money for a young boy who needs an operation.

The movie was filmed in Paris. It showed how parkour can be used to get around a city very fast.

Then, in 2003, a UK documentary was released called *Jump London*.

The documentary was filmed all over London. It showed some of London's most impressive buildings and famous places.

Practising parkour in London

After *Jump London* was released, parkour became huge around the world.

Now, parkour appears in major Hollywood movies.

Casino Royale

Parkour was used in the opening scene of the James Bond movie *Casino Royale*.

James Bond chases a villain through a city and across roofs and cranes. It was an explosive opening to the movie!

REMEMBER

The incredible moves you see in movies, magazines and books are performed by trained professionals.

Parkour is a stunning visual art. It has been featured in music videos and magazine and TV adverts.

Parkour has been used to advertise clothes, phones and cars.

A New York photoshoot for clothing company, Ecko.

This photograph is from a photoshoot for a German magazine. Parkour practitioners showed off their moves while wearing clothes from top designers.

Fashion companies always like to show off their designs in a dynamic way!

CHAPTER 7 **PARKOUR VISION**

Practicing parkour will change your way of seeing the buildings and area around you.

You begin to see new ways of moving through a city or a park.

You see new ways of using the buildings and objects around you.

Your vision changes completely!

CHAPTER 8

A WAY OF LIFE

For those who practise parkour it becomes more than just a sport or a hobby.

It changes your way of thinking about yourself and the place where you live.

Parkour helps you improve
physically and mentally every day.

Parkour becomes a way of
life for its practitioners.
They learn that they can
overcome problems
in their life – not only
in training!

NEED TO KNOW WORDS

adrenaline A substance produced in the body in response to excitement. It makes your heart beat faster.

discipline The ability to commit to practising and training regularly and with focus.

documentary A factual TV show or movie.

founder A person who starts something, such as an organisation or a sport.

impact The force that goes through your body when you land from a jump.

obstacle A wall, park bench, set of steps – anything you can move over when practising parkour.

potential What your mind and body are capable of if you train hard.

practise This word can be used in two ways. It can mean when a person takes part in an activity. It can also mean doing something again and again to improve.

practitioner A person who practises (takes part) in an activity.

precision Being very accurate with your movements and landings from jumps.

technique A way of doing something.

vault A movement that allows you to move over an obstacle and keep moving.

vision The ability to see new possibilities for movement in your surroundings.

LEARNING PARKOUR

If you want to practise parkour it is best to learn from a qualified teacher or an experienced practitioner.

• For help on joining classes, go to *www.parkourgenerations.com*. You will find information on groups and classes in your community.

• All you need to take part are running shoes and simple training clothes such as sportswear – nothing else!

• Classes always involve tough physical training and lots of practise of the movements of parkour. It can be hard work!

Dan Edwardes teaches a parkour class

PARKOUR ONLINE

Websites

http://www.parkourgenerations.com/
Information about parkour and where to find classes

http://www.majesticforce.com/
More great parkour information

http://www.kiell.com/
Great parkour photographs

INDEX